CHRISTMAS PRAYLUDES

Eight Reflective Organ...

Arranged by RUTH ELAINE SC...

Editor: Dale Tucker
Art Design: Olivia D. Novak

CONTENTS

LIFT UP YOUR HEADS, YE MIGHTY GATES

TRURO

SW: Principals 8', 4', 2', Mixture, Reed 8'
GT: Principals 8', 4', 2', Sw. to Gt.
CH: Solo Trumpet 8'
PED: Principals 16', 8', 4', Sw. to Ped.

Psalmodia Evangelica, 1789
Arranged by RUTH ELAINE SCHRAM

With authority (♩ = ca. 94-100)

A little more broadly

O COME, O COME, EMMANUEL
VENI EMMANUEL

SW: Flute 8', String Celeste 8'
GT: Diapason 8'
CH: Flutes 8', 4', Sw. to Ch.
PED: Soft 16', 8', Sw. to Ped.

15th CENTURY FRENCH CAROL
Arranged by RUTH ELAINE SCHRAM

With freedom (♩ = ca. 88)

GBM0203

GBM0203

9

GBM0203

COME, THOU LONG-EXPECTED JESUS

HYFRYDOL

SW: Trumpet 8'
GT: Principals 8', 4', Ch. to Gt.
CH: Principal 8', Flutes 8', 4'
PED: 16', 8', (4')

ROWLAND H. PRICHARD, 1830
Arranged by RUTH ELAINE SCHRAM

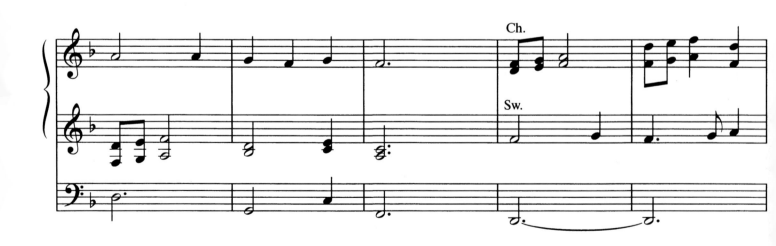

optional 1st ending

Ch.

rit.

mf a tempo

Sw.

Gt.

cresc.
Ch.

ANGELS SING!

Medley including: "Angels from the Realms of Glory" (Regent Square)
"Hark the Herald Angels Sing" (Mendelssohn)
and "Angels We Have Heard on High" (Gloria)

SW: Flutes 8', 4', 2'
GT: Principals 8', 4', Sw. to Gt.
PED: 16', 8'

Arranged by
RUTH ELAINE SCHRAM

INFANT HOLY, INFANT LOWLY
W ZLOBIE LEZY

SW: Flutes 8', 4', String and Celeste 8'
GT: Flutes 8', 4', Sw. to Gt.
PED: Soft Solo Reed 4' (trem.)

TRADITIONAL POLISH CAROL
Arranged by RUTH ELAINE SCHRAM

WHAT CHILD IS THIS
GREENSLEEVES

SW: Cornet
GT: Flutes 8', 4'
PED: Soft 16', 8'

16th CENTURY ENGLISH MELODY
Arranged by RUTH ELAINE SCHRAM

Flowing (♩ = 92)

optional repeat to m.1

optional Fine

mp

Gt. add Sw. St. 8', 4'

rit.

mf *a tempo*

optional repeat to m.57

(play cued notes if repeating)

Opening Registration
Sw.

p   rit.
Gt.

add Soft 32'

O COME, ALL YE FAITHFUL
ADESTE FIDELES

SW: Principals 8', 4', 2'
GT: Principals 8', 4', 2'
PED: Principals 16', 8', Gt. to Ped.

JOHN F. WADE, 1743
Arranged by RUTH ELAINE SCHRAM

JOY TO THE WORLD
ANTIOCH

SW: Principals 8', 4', 2', Reed 8'
GT: Principals 8', 4', 2', Sw. to Gt.
CH: Solo Reed 8'
PED: Principals 16', 8', 4', Mixture, Gt. to Ped.

GEORGE FRIDERIC HANDEL, 174
Arranged by RUTH ELAINE SCHRAM

GBM0203

34

GBM0203

Selections from the
Saint Cecilia Organ Series

Printed in USA AD311B

Collections of Hymn Tune Arrangements for Organ

The Roberta Bitgood Organ Album
by Roberta Bitgood
____ (GB00675)

A Collection of Hymns
by Alfred Fedak
____ (DM9601)

The Crystal Cathedral Organ Collection
by Robert Hebble
____ (EL9508)

Eight Hymntune Preludes
by David Lasky
____ (GB00698)

Eight Preludes on Old Southern Hymn Tunes
by Gardner Read
____ (GB00293)

Eleven Chorale Preludes on Hymn Tunes
arranged by James D. Kimball
____ (EL03914)

Favorite Hymns for Organ
by Robert Hebble
____ (BHS9501) $8.95

Festive Hymns & Pieces
by Robert Hebble
____ (GB9502)

Festive Hymns and Pieces
by James Pethel
____ (GB00696)

Five Improvisations on Communion Hymns
by David Lasky
____ (GB00702) $5.50

Four Preludes on English Hymn Tunes
by Matthew H. Corl
____ (GB9501)

Four Preludes on Favorite American Hymns
arranged by Rulon Christiansen
____ (BHS00002)

Four Preludes on Welsh Hymn Tunes
by Theodore W. Ripper
____ (GB00678)

Gospel Meditations for Organ
by Jon Spong
____ (BHS9601)

Hymns for the Church Year
by James Pethel
____ (BHS9502)

Hymns of Faith
by Jack W. Jones
____ (BHS9602)

Hymns of Praise
by Joyce Jones
____ (BHS9603)

In Quiet Joy
by Darwin Wolford
____ (EL9501)

The Alice Jordan Collection of Hymn Tunes for Organ
by Alice Jordan
____ (DM00261) Volume I
____ (DM00263) Volume II

Meditations on Communion Hymns
by Leo Sowerby
____ (GB00320)

Music for Organ
by Calvin Hampton
____ (DM00266)

Nine Hymn Preludes
by Stephen Weber
____ (GB9516) Volume I
____ (GB9610) Volume II

Organ Preludes on Favorite Hymns
by Joyce Jones
____ (EL96109)

Organ Variations and Voluntaries (Nine Hymn Tune Compositions)
by Jon Spong
____ (GB00693)

Prayludes (Reflective Settings of Favorite Hymns)
by Ruth Elaine Schram
____ (BHS9701)

Preludes for 55 Well-Known Hymn Tunes
by Howard McKinney
____ (FE09770)

Preludes, Meditations, and Quiet Postludes
arranged by Robert Graham
____ (F2892AOX)

Preludes with Hymn Quotes
by Walter W. Schurr
____ (BHS9702)

Six Chorale Preludes
by Dudley Buck, ed. Barbara Owen
____ (DM9503)

Ten Hymn Preludes in Trio Style
by David Harris
____ (GB00632) Set 1

Three Communion Meditations on Ancient Hymns
by Michael A. Joseph
____ (GB00685)

Twelve Chorale Improvisations
by Lindsay Lafford
____ (GB9603)

Twelve Hymn Preludes
by Seth Bingham
____ (GB00151) Set 1
____ (GB00152) Set 2

Twelve Hymn Preludes
by James Pethel
____ (EL03930)

Twelve Hymn Settings
by David N. Johnson
____ (SCHBK07634)

Twelve Improvisations on Hymns
by Michael Joseph
____ (GB9505)

Variations on Four Sunday School Tunes
by Virgil Thomson
____ (GB00648)

Hymn Introduction and Accompaniment Collections

from Warner Bros. Publications

These hymn accompaniment and introduction books will enhance any worship service with little effort from the organist. Select from these best-selling collections, available only from Warner Bros. Publications. Your hymn playing will never be better.

INTRODUCTIONS

**Eight Fanfare Introductions
to Popular Christmas Hymns**
by James Jacka Coyle

GBM0008

Fourteen Introductions on Christmas Carols
by Jerry Westenkuehler
GBM0101

Seven Majestic Hymn Introductions
by Jerry Westenkuehler
GB9604—Volume I
GB9707—Volume II
GBM0005—Volume III

BEST SELLERS

**Ten Introductions on Hymns for Advent,
Christmas, and Epiphany**
by David Lasky
GB9608—Volume I
GB9702—Volume II

Twenty Intonations on Festive Hymns
by David Lasky
GB9609—Volume I
GB9904—Volume II

VERSE ACCOMPANIMENTS

**Free Accompaniments and Descants
to Twelve Familiar Hymns for Organ**
by Hal H. Hopson
GB00650

Free Organ Accompaniments to Fifty Hymns
by T. Tertius Noble
FE08430

**Free Organ Accompaniments
to One Hundred Well-Known Hymn Tunes**
by T. Tertius Noble
FE08175

**Hymn Accompaniments
for Congregational Singing**
by Daniel E. Gawthrop
GB00657—Volume I
GB00697—Volume II

Printed in USA   AD343A